CUPID'S ARROW

Cupid's Arrow

LOVE POEMS

EDITED BY

Robin Langley Sommer

Grange BOOKS

Published by Grange Books
An Imprint of Grange Books PLC
Units 1–6, Industrial Estate
Hoo, near Rochester
Kent ME3 9ND

This edition published 1999

Produced in association with Saraband Inc.

Front cover painting based on Bougereau's
"The First Kiss" MARY EVANS PICTURE LIBRARY

ISBN: 1-84013-246-9

Printed in China

9 8 7 6 5 4 3 2 1

For

Rachel and Nick

Two hearts—
Entwined in earthly joy,
Bonded in deepest sorrow,
Blessed with the miracle of love.

Foreword

The poetry of passion takes many forms and speaks to many kinds of love. Its power to stir kindred feelings testifies to our need for poets and their songs down through the ages. Who does not respond to such lines as Emily Dickinson's "Parting is all we know of heaven/And all we need of hell"? Or to the words of the Persian poet Hafiz: "The lips of the one I love are my perpetual pleasure:/The Lord be praised, for my heart's desire is attained."

One constant theme in the poetry of love is passion's power to make time stand still—if only for an hour. The intensity of the experience, the dissolution of that gnawing sense of apartness that poets and mystics put into words for us, make physical love a kind of window on eternity. By the same token, love thwarted or betrayed turns to bitterness and grief of the deepest kind, and the poetry of love is almost equally the poetry of loss. Running through, beneath, and between the lines of the most fervent lyric is the sense of urgency—the sense that beauty and youth are transitory, that time is the enemy of ardor. Rare is the poet (or the more prosaic person) in whom passion strikes deep roots and grows into the kind of love described in Anne Bradstreet's poem "To My Dear and Loving Husband." In the end, it is no coincidence that the word "passion" stands for both consuming love and deepest pain. Perhaps, at the heart of experience, the two are one.

Contents

III. Chimeras

IV. Closings

I

Awakenings

The First Day

I wish I could remember the first day,
First hour, first moment of your meeting me;
If bright or dim the season, it might be
Summer or winter for aught I can say.
So unrecorded did it slip away,
So blind was I to see and to foresee,
So dull to mark the budding of my tree
That would not blossom yet for many a May.
If only I could recollect it! Such
A day of days! I let it come and go
As traceless as a thaw of bygone snow.
It seemed to mean so little, meant so much!
If only now I could recall that touch,
First touch of hand in hand!—Did one but know!

CHRISTINA ROSSETTI

The Progress of Love

Beneath the myrtle's secret shade,
  When Delia blessed my eyes;
At first I viewed the lovely maid
  In silent soft surprise.
With trembling voice, and anxious mind,
  I softly whispered love;
She blushed a smile so sweetly kind,
  Did all my fears remove.
Her lovely yielding form I pressed,
  Sweet maddening kisses stole;
And soon her swimming eyes confessed
  The wishes of her soul:
In wild tumultuous bliss, I cry,
  'O Delia, now be kind!'
She pressed me close, and with a sigh,
  To melting joys resigned.

ROBERT DODSLEY

from Epithalamion (Wedding Song)

Wake now, my love, awake; for it is time.
The Rosy Morne long since left Tithones bed,
All ready to her silver coche to clyme,
And Phoebus gins to shew his glorious hed.
Hark how the cheereful birds do chaunt theyr laies
And carroll of Loves praise.
The merry Larke hir mattins sings aloft,
The Thrush replyes, the Mavis descant playes;
The Ouzell shrills; the Ruddock warbles soft;
So goodly all agree with sweet consent,
To this dayes merriment.
Ah! my deere love, why doe ye sleepe thus long?
When meeter were that ye should now awake,
T'awayt the comming of your joyous make,
And hearken to the birds lovelearnèd song,
The deawy leaves among.
For they of joy and pleasance to you sing,
That all the woods them answer and theyr eccho
ring.

My love is now awake out of her dreame,
And her fayre eyes, like stars that dimmèd were
With darksome cloud, now shew theyr goodly
beams

More bright then Hesperus his head doth rere.
Come now, ye damzels, daughters of delight,
Helpe quickly her to dight,
But first come ye fayre houres, which were begot
In Joves sweet paradice of Day and Night,
Which doe the seasons of the yeare allot,
And al that ever in this world is fayre
Doe make and still repayre.
And ye three handmayds of the Cyprian Queene,
The which doe still adorne her beauties pride,
Helpe to addorne my beautifullest bride:
And as ye her array, still throw betweene
Some graces to be seene,
And as ye use to Venus, to her sing,
The whiles the woods shal answer, and your eccho
ring.

EDMUND SPENSER

To The Virgins, To Make Much of Time

Gather ye rosebuds while ye may,
  Old Time is still a-flying:
And this same flower that smiles today
  Tomorrow will be dying.

The glorious lamp of heaven, the sun,
The higher he's a-getting,
The sooner will his race be run,
And nearer he's to setting.

That age is best which is the first,
  When youth and blood are warmer;
But being spent, the worse, and worst
  Times still succeed the former.

Then be not coy, but use your time,
  And while ye may, go marry:
For having lost but once your prime,
  You may for ever tarry.

ROBERT HERRICK

Love's Emblems

Now the lusty spring is seen;
  Golden yellow, gaudy blue,
  Daintily invite the view:
Everywhere on every green
Roses blushing as they blow
  And enticing men to pull,
Lilies whiter than the snow,
  Woodbines of sweet honey full:
    All love's emblems, and all cry,
    'Ladies, if not plucked, we die.'

Yet the lusty spring hath stayed;
  Blushing red and purest white
  Daintily to love invite
Every woman, every maid:
Cherries kissing as they grow,
  And inviting men to taste,
Apples even ripe below,
  Winding gently to the waist:
    All love's emblems, and all cry,
    'Ladies, if not plucked, we die.'

JOHN FLETCHER

She Walks in Beauty

She walks in beauty, like the night
  Of cloudless climes and starry skies;
And all that's best of dark and bright
  Meet in her aspect and her eyes:
Thus mellowed to that tender light
  Which heaven to gaudy day denies.

One shade the more, one ray the less,
  Had half impaired the nameless grace
Which waves in every raven tress,
  Or softly lightens o'er her face;
Where thoughts serenely sweet express
  How pure, how dear their dwelling place.
And on that cheek, and o'er that brow,
  So soft, so calm, yet eloquent,
The smiles that win, the tints that glow,
  But tell of days in goodness spent,
A mind at peace with all below,
  A heart whose love is innocent!

GEORGE GORDON, LORD BYRON

The Passionate Shepherd to His Love

Come live with me and be my Love,
And we will all the pleasures prove
That hills and valleys, dales and fields,
Or woods or steepy mountain yields.

And we will sit upon the rocks,
And see the shepherds feed their flocks
By shallow rivers, to whose falls
Melodious birds sing madrigals.

And I will make thee beds of roses
And a thousand fragrant posies;
A cap of flowers, and a kirtle
Embroidered all with leaves of myrtle.

A gown made of the finest wool
Which from our pretty lambs we pull;
Fair-linèd slippers for the cold,
With buckles of the purest gold.

A belt of straw and ivy-buds
With coral clasps and amber studs:
And if these pleasures may thee move,
Come live with me and be my Love.

The shepherd swains shall dance and sing
For thy delight each May morning:
If these delights thy mind may move,
Then live with me and be my Love.

CHRISTOPHER MARLOWE

On a Rosebud Sent to Her Lover

The tender bud within herself doth close
with secret sweetness till it prove a rose;
And then as fit for profit as for pleasure
Yields sweet content to him that gains the treasure:

So she that sent this, yet a bud unblown,
In time may prove a rose, and be your own.

ANON

II

Flowerings

Elegy V

In summer's heat and mid-time of the day
To rest my limbs upon a bed I lay,
One window shut, the other open stood,
Which gave such light, as twinkles in a wood,
Like twilight glimpse at setting of the sun,
Or night being past, and yet not day begun.
Such light to shamefast maidens must be shown,
Where they must sport, and seem to be unknown.
Then came Corinna in a long loose gown,
Her white neck hid with tresses hanging down:
Resembling fair Semiramis going to bed
Or Layis of a thousand wooers sped.
I snatched her gown, being thin, the harm was small,
Yet strived she to be covered there withal.
And striving thus as one that would be cast,
Betrayed herself, and yielded at the last.
Stark naked as she stood before mine eye,
Not one wen in her body could I spy.
What arms and shoulders did I touch and see,
How apt her breasts were to be pressed by me.
How smooth a belly under her waist saw I?
How large a leg, and what a lusty thigh?
To leave the rest, all liked me passing well,
I clinged her naked body, down she fell,

Judge you the rest, being tired she bade me kiss,
Jove send me more such afternoons as this.

OVID

from Canto XXX, "Purgatory"
The Divine Comedy

I have beheld, ere now, at break of day,
The eastern clime all roseate; and the sky
Opposed, one deep and beautiful serene;
And the sun's face so shaded, and with mists
Attemper'd, at his rising, that the eye
Long while endured the sight: thus, in a cloud
Of flowers, that from those hands angelic rose,
And down within and about the chariot
Fell showering, in white veil with olive wreathed,
A virgin in my view appear'd, beneath
Green mantle, robed in hue of living flame:
And o'er my spirit, that so long a time
Had from her presence felt no shuddering dread,
Albeit mine eyes discern'd her not, there moved
A hidden virtue from her, at whose touch
The power of ancient love was strong within me.

DANTE

The Sun Rising

Busy old fool, unruly Sun,
Why dost thou thus,
Through windows and through curtains call on us?
Must to thy motions lovers' seasons run?
Saucy pedantic wretch, go chide
Late school-boys, and sour 'prentices,
  Go tell court-huntsmen that the King will ride,
  Call country ants to harvest offices;
Love, all alike, no season knows, nor clime,
Nor hours, days, months, which are the rags of time.

Thy beams, so reverend and strong
Why shouldst thou think?
I could eclipse and cloud them with a wink,
But that I would not lose her sight so long:
If her eyes have not blinded thine,
Look, and tomorrow late tell me,
  Whether both the Indias of spice and mine
  Be where thou left'st them, or lie here with me.
Ask for those kings whom thou saw'st yesterday,
And thou shalt hear, 'All here in one bed lay.'

She's all States, and all Princes I;
Nothing else is.
Princes do but play us; compared to this,
All honour's mimic; all wealth alchemy.

Thou, Sun, art half as happy as we,
In that the world's contracted thus;
  Thine age asks ease, and since thy duties be
  To warm the world, that's done in warming us.
Shine here to us, and thou art everywhere;
This bed thy centre is, these walls thy sphere.

JOHN DONNE

Sonnet XLIII, from The Portuguese

How do I love thee? Let me count the ways.
I love thee to the depth and breadth and height
My soul can reach, when feeling out of sight
For the ends of Being and ideal Grace.
I love thee to the level of every day's
Most quiet need, by sun and candlelight.
I love thee freely, as men strive for Right;
I love thee purely, as they turn from Praise.
I love thee with the passion put to use
In my old griefs, and with my childhood's faith.
I love thee with a love I seemed to lose
With my lost saints,—I love thee with the breath,
Smiles, tears, of all my life!—and, if God choose,
I shall but love thee better after death.

ELIZABETH BARRETT BROWNING

To Helen

Helen, thy beauty is to me
Like those Nicéan barks of yore,
That gently, o'er a perfumed sea,
The weary, way-worn wanderer bore
To his own native shore.

On desperate seas long wont to roam,
Thy hyacinth hair, thy classic face,
Thy naiad airs have brought me home
To the glory that was Greece
And the grandeur that was Rome.

Lo! in yon brilliant window niche
How statuelike I see thee stand,
The agate lamp within thy hand!
Ah, Psyche, from the regions which
Are holy land!

EDGAR ALLEN POE

Sonnet 18

Shall I compare thee to a summer's day?
Thou art more lovely and more temperate:
Rough winds do shake the darling buds of May,
And summer's lease hath all too short a date:
Sometime too hot the eye of heaven shines,
And often is his gold complexion dimmed;
And every fair from fair sometime declines,
By chance, or nature's changing course untrimmed;
But thy eternal summer shall not fade,
Nor lose possession of that fair thou owest,
Nor shall death brag thou wanderest in his shade,
When in eternal lines to time thou growest;
So long as men can breathe, or eyes can see,
So long lives this, and this gives life to thee.

WILLIAM SHAKESPEARE

Ask me no more where Jove bestows
When June is past, the fading rose;
For in your beauty's orient deep
These flowers, as in their causes, sleep.
Ask me no more whither do stray
The golden atoms of the day;
For in pure love Heaven did prepare
Those powders to enrich your hair.

Ask me no more whither doth haste
The nightingale when May is past,
For in your sweet dividing throat
She winters, and keeps warm her note.

Ask me no more when those stars' light
That downwards fall in dead of night;
For in your eyes they sit, and there
Fixed become as in their sphere.

Ask me no more if East or West
The phoenix builds her spicy nest;
For unto you at last she flies,
And in your fragrant bosom dies.

THOMAS CAREW

Love

As some dark stream within a cavern's breast,
Flows murmuring, moaning for the distant sun,
So ere I met thee, murmuring its unrest,
Did my life's current coldly, darkly run.
And as that stream, beneath the sun's full gaze,
Its separate course and life no more maintains,
But now absorbed, transfused, far o'er the plains,
It floats, etherealized in those warm rays;
So in the sunlight of thy fervid love,
My heart, so long to earth's dark channels given,
Now soars, all pain, all doubt, all ill above,
And breathes the ether of the upper heaven:
So thy high spirit holds and governs mine;
So is my life, my being, lost in thine.

ANNE LYNCH BOTTA

Sonnet VII: Beauty, Time, and Love

Let others sing of Knights and Paladines
In agèd accents and untimely words,
Paint shadows in imaginary lines,
Which well the reach of their high wit records:
But I must sing of thee, and those fair eyes
Authentic shall my verse in time to come;
When yet th' unborn shall say, *Lo, where she lies!*
Whose beauty made him speak, that else was dumb!
These are the arcs, the trophies I erect,
That fortify thy name against old age;
And these thy sacred virtues must protect
Against the Dark, and Time's consuming rage.
  Though th' error of my youth in them appear,
  Suffice, they show I lived, and loved thee dear.

SAMUEL DANIELS

To Celia

Drink to me only with thine eyes,
And I will pledge with mine;
Or leave a kiss but in the cup
And I'll not look for wine.
The thirst that from the soul doth rise
Doth ask a drink divine;
But might I of Jove's nectar sup,
I would not change for thine.
I sent thee late a rosy wreath,
Not so much honouring thee
As giving it a hope that there
It could not withered be;
But thou thereon didst only breathe,
And sent'st it back to me;
Since when it grows, and smells, I swear,
Not of itself but thee!

BEN JONSON

To My Dear and Loving Husband

If ever two were one, then surely we.
If ever man were lov'd by wife, then thee;
If ever wife was happy in a man,
Compare with me ye women if you can.
I prize thy love more then whole Mines of gold,
Or all the riches that the East doth hold.
My love is such that Rivers cannot quench,
Nor ought but love from thee, give recompense.
Thy love is such I can no way repay,
The heavens reward thee manifold I pray.
Then while we live, in love lets so persever,
That when we live no more, we may live ever.

ANNE BRADSTREET

Cherry-ripe

There is a garden in her face
  Where roses and white lilies blow;
A heavenly paradise is that place,
  Wherein all pleasant fruits do flow:
    There cherries grow which none may buy
    Till 'Cherry-ripe' themselves do cry.

Those cherries fairly do enclose
  Of orient pearls a double row,
Which when her lovely laughter shows,
  They look like rose-buds filled with snow;
    Yet them nor peer nor prince can buy
    Till 'Cherry-ripe' themselves do cry.

Her eyes like angels watch them still;
  Her brows like bended bows do stand,
Threatening with piercing frowns to kill
  All that attempt with eye or hand
    Those sacred cherries to come nigh,
    Till 'Cherry-ripe' themselves do cry.

THOMAS CAMPION

The Good Morrow

I wonder by my troth, what thou and I
  Did, till we loved? were we not weaned till then?
But sucked on country pleasures, childishly?
  Or snorted we i' the seven sleepers' den?
'Twas so; But this, all pleasures fancies be.
If ever any beauty I did see,
Which I desired, and got, 'twas but a dream of thee.

And now good morrow to our waking souls,
  Which watch not one another out of fear;
For love, all love of other sights controls,
  And makes one little room, an everywhere.

Let sea-discoverers to new worlds have gone,
Let maps to others, worlds on worlds have shown,
Let us possess our world, each hath one, and is one.

My face in thine eye, thine in mine appears,
  And true plain hearts do in the faces rest,
Where can we find two better hemispheres
  Without sharp North, without declining West?
Whatever dies, was not mixed equally;
If our two loves be one, or, thou and I
Love so alike, that none do slacken, none can die.

JOHN DONNE

from In a Gondola

HE SINGS

I send my heart up to thee, all my heart
  In this my singing.
For the stars help me, and the sea bears part;
  The very night is clinging
Closer to Venice' streets to leave one space
  Above me, whence thy face
May light my joyous heart to thee its
    dwelling-place.

* * *

SHE SINGS

The moth's kiss, first!
Kiss me as if you made believe
You were not sure, this eve
How my face, your flower, had pursed
Its petals up; so here and there
You brush it, till I grow aware
Who wants me, and wide ope I burst.

ROBERT BROWNING

Go lovely rose—
Tell her that wastes her time and me,
That now she knows,
When I resemble her to thee,
How sweet and fair she seems to be.

Tell her that's young,
And shuns to have her graces spied,
That hadst thou sprung
In deserts where no men abide,
Thou must have uncommended died.

Small is the worth
Of beauty from the light retired:
Bid her come forth,
Suffer herself to be desired,
And not blush so to be admired.

Then die—that she
The common fate of all things rare
May read in thee;
How small a part of time they share
That are so wondrous sweet and fair!

EDMUND WALLER

Did Not

'Twas a new feeling—something more
Than we had dared to own before,
  Which then we hid not;
We saw it in each other's eye,
And wished, in every half-breathed sigh,
  To speak, but did not.

She felt my lips' impassioned touch—
'Twas the first time I dared so much,
  And yet she chid not;
But whispered o'er my burning brow,
'Oh, do you doubt I love you now?'
  Sweet soul! I did not.

Warmly I felt her bosom thrill,
I pressed it closer, closer still,
  Though gently bid not;
Till—oh! the world hath seldom heard
Of lovers, who so nearly erred,
  And yet, who did not.

THOMAS MOORE

Meeting at Night

I

The grey sea and the long black land;
And the yellow half-moon large and low;
And the startled little waves that leap
In fiery ringlets from their sleep,
As I gain the cove with pushing prow,
And quench its speed i' the slushy sand.

II

Then a mile of warm sea-scented beach;
Three fields to cross till a farm appears;
A tap at the pane, the quick sharp scratch
And blue spurt of a lighted match,
And a voice less loud, thro' its joys and fears,
Than the two hearts beating each to each!

ROBERT BROWNING

III

Chimeras

My mistress' eyes are nothing like the sun;
Coral is far more red than her lips' red:
If snow be white, why then her breasts are dun;
If hairs be wires, black wires grow on her head.
I have seen roses damasked, red and white,
But no such roses see I in her cheeks;
And in some perfumes is there more delight
Than in the breath that from my mistress reeks.
I love to hear her speak; yet well I know
That music hath a far more pleasing sound:
I grant I never saw a goddess go,
My mistress, when she walks, treads on the ground:
And yet, by heaven, I think my love as rare
As any she belied with false compare.

WILLIAM SHAKESPEARE

Renouncement

I must not think of thee; and, tired yet strong,
I shun the thought that lurks in all delight—
The thought of thee— and in the blue heaven's height,
And in the sweetest passage of a song.
Oh, just beyond the fairest thoughts that throng
This breast, the thought of thee waits hidden yet bright;
But it must never, never come in sight;
I must stop short of thee the whole day long.

But when sleep comes to close each difficult day,
When night gives pause to the long watch I keep,
And all my bonds I needs must loose apart,
Must doff my will as raiment laid away,—
With the first dream that comes with the first sleep
I run, I run, I am gathered to thy heart.

ALICE MEYNELL

from The Question

Methought that of these visionary flowers
  I made a nosegay, bound in such a way
That in the same hues, which in their natural bow-
  ers
  Were mingled or opposed, the like array
Kept these imprisoned children of the Hours
  Within my hand,—and then, elate and gay,
I hastened to the spot whence I had come,
That I might there present it!—Oh! to whom?

PERCY BYSSHE SHELLEY

An Hour With Thee

An hour with thee! When earliest day
Dapples with gold the eastern grey,
Oh, what can frame my mind to bear
The toil and turmoil, cark and care,
New griefs, which coming hours unfold,
And sad remembrance of the old?
One hour with thee.

One hour with thee! When burning June
Waves his red flag at pitch of noon;
What shall repay the faithful swain,
His labour on the sultry plain;
And, more than cave or sheltering bough,
Cool feverish blood and throbbing brow?
One hour with thee.

One hour with thee! When sun is set,
Oh, what can teach me to forget
The thankless labours of the day;
The hopes, the wishes, flung away;
The increasing wants, and lessening gains,
The master's pride, who scorns my pains?
One hour with thee.

SIR WALTER SCOTT

The Dream

All trembling in my arms Aminta lay,
Defending of the bliss I strove to take;
Raising my rapture by her kind delay,
Her force so charming was and weak.
The soft resistance did betray the grant,
While I pressed on the heaven of my desires;
Her rising breasts with nimbler motions pant;
Her dying eyes assume new fires.
Now to the height of languishment she grows,
And still her looks new charms put on;
– Now the last mystery of Love she knows,
We sigh, and kiss: I waked, and all was done.

'Twas but a dream, yet by my heart I knew,
Which still was panting, part of it was true:
Oh how I strove the rest to have believed;
Ashamed and angry to be undeceived!

APHRA BEHN

Out upon it, I have loved
  Three whole days together;
And am like to love three more,
  If it hold fair weather.

Time shall moult away his wings
  Ere he shall discover
In the whole wide world again
  Such a constant lover.

But a pox upon't, no praise
  There is due at all to me:
Love with me had made no stays,
  Had it any been but she.

Had it any been but she
  And that very very face,
There had been at least ere this
  A dozen dozen in her place.

SIR JOHN SUCKLING

To His Coy Mistress

Had we but world enough, and time,
This coyness, Lady, were no crime.
We would sit down and think which way
To walk and pass our long love's day.
Thou by the Indian Ganges' side
Shouldst rubies find: I by the tide
Of Humber would complain. I would
Love you ten years before the Flood,
And you should, if you please, refuse
Till the conversion of the Jews.
My vegetable love should grow
Vaster than empires, and more slow;
An hundred years should go to praise
Thine eyes and on thy forehead gaze;
Two hundred to adore each breast;
But thirty thousand to the rest;
An age at least to every part,
And the last age should show your heart;
For, Lady, you deserve this state,
Nor would I love at lower rate.
  But at my back I always hear
Time's winged chariot hurrying near;
And yonder all before us lie
Deserts of vast eternity

Thy beauty shall no more be found,
Nor, in they marble vault, shall sound
My echoing song: then worms shall try
That long preserved virginity,
And your quaint honour turn to dust,
And into ashes all my lust:
The grave's a fine and private place,
But none, I think, do there embrace.
  Now therefore, while the youthful hue
Sits on thy skin like morning dew,
And while thy willing soul transpires
At every pore with instant fires,
Now let us sport us while we may,
And now, like amorous birds of prey,
Rather at once our time devour
Than languish in his slow-chapt power.
Let us roll all our strength and all
Our sweetness up into one ball,
And tear our pleasures with rough strife
Thorough the iron gates of life:
Thus, though we cannot make our sun
Stand still, yet we will make him run.

ANDREW MARVELL

To Marguerite—Continued

Yes! in the sea of life enisled,
With echoing straits between us thrown,
Dotting the shoreless watery wild,
We mortal millions live *alone*.
The islands feel the enclasping flow,
And then their endless bounds they know.

But when the moon their hollows lights,
And they are swept by balms of spring,
And in their glens, on starry nights,
The nightingales divinely sing;
And lovely notes, from shore to shore,
Across the sounds and channels pour—

O! then a longing like despair
Is to their farthest caverns sent;
For surely once, they feel, we were
Parts of a single continent!
Now round us spreads the watery plain—
O might our marges meet again!

Who ordered that their longing's fire
Should be, as soon as kindled, cooled?
Who renders vain their deep desire?—

A God, a God their severance ruled!
And bade betwixt their shores to be
The unplumbed, salt, estranging sea.

MATTHEW ARNOLD

With how sad steps, O moon, thou climb'st the skies!
How silently, and with how wan a face!
What! may it be that even in heavenly place
That busy archer his sharp arrows tries?
Sure, if that long-with-love-acquainted eyes
Càn judge of love, thou feel'st a lover's case
I read it in thy looks; thy languished grace
To me, that feel the like, thy state descries.
Then, even of fellowship, O Moon, tell me,
Is constant love deemed there but want of wit?
Are beauties there as proud as here they be?
Do they above love to be loved, and yet
Those lovers scorn whom that love doth possess?
Do they call 'virtue' there— ungratefulness?

SIR PHILIP SIDNEY

To Fanny (Sonnet XLIV)

I cry your mercy—pity—love!—aye, love!
Merciful love that tantalises not,
One-thoughted, never-wandering, guileless love,
Unmask'd, and being seen—without a blot!
O! let me have thee whole,—all—all—be mine!
That shape, that fairness, that sweet minor zest
Of love, your kiss,—those hands, those eyes divine,
That warm, white, lucent, million-pleasured breast,—
Yourself, your soul—in pity give me all,
Withhold no atom's atom or I die,
Or living on perhaps, your wretched thrall,
Forget, in the midst of idle misery,
Life's purposes,—the palate of my mind
Losing its gust, and my ambition blind!

JOHN KEATS

IV

Closings

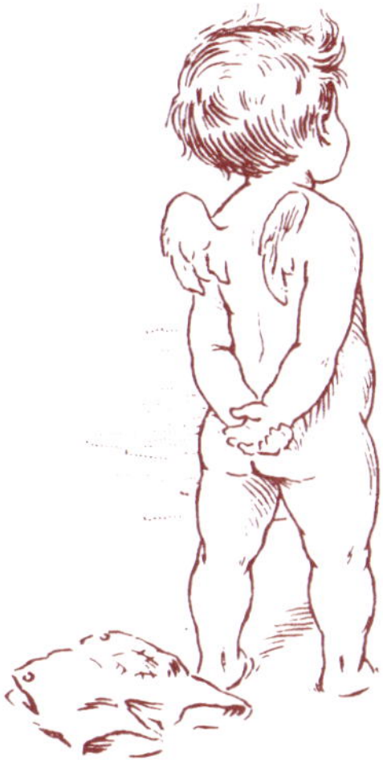

Mother, I cannot mind my wheel;
My fingers ache, my lips are dry;
Oh! if you felt the pain I feel!
But oh, who ever felt as I!

SAPPHO
TRANS. WALTER SAVAGE LANDOR

Since there's no help, come let us kiss and part—
Nay, I have done, you get no more of me;
And I am glad, yea, glad with all my heart,
That thus so cleanly I myself can free.
Shake hands for ever, cancel all our vows,
And when we meet at any time again,
Be it not seen in either of our brows
That we one jot of former love retain.
Now at the last gasp of Love's latest breath,
When, his pulse failing, Passion speechless lies,
When Faith is kneeling by his bed of death,
And Innocence is closing up his eyes,
— Now if thou would'st, when all have given him over,
From death to life thou might'st him yet recover.

MICHAEL DRAYTON

A Red Red Rose

O my Luve's like a red, red rose,
  That's newly sprung in June;
O my Luve's like the melodie
  That's sweetly play'd in tune.—

As fair art thou, my bonie lass,
  So deep in luve am I;
And I will love thee still, my Dear,
  Till a' the seas gang dry.—

Till a' the seas gang dry, my Dear,
  And the rocks melt wi' the sun:
I will love thee still, my Dear,
  While the sands o' life shall run.—

And fare thee weel, my only Luve!
  And fare thee weel, a while!
And I will come again, my Luve,
  Tho' it were ten thousand mile!

ROBERT BURNS

The Welcome

Go, let the fatted calf be killed;
  My Prodigal's come home at last;
With noble resolutions filled,
  And filled with sorrow for the past.
  No more will burn with love or wine:
But quite has left his women and his swine.

Welcome, ah welcome my poor Heart;
  Welcome; I little thought, I'll swear,
('Tis now so long since we did part)
  Ever again to see thee here:
  Dear Wanderer, since from me you fled,
How often have I heard that thou wert dead!

Hast thou not found each woman's breast
  (The lands where thou hast travelled)
Either by savages possessed,
  Or wild, and uninhabited?
  What joy could'st take, or what repose
In countries so uncivilized as those?

Lust, the scorching Dog-star, here
  Rages with immoderate heat;
Whilst Pride the rugged Northern Bear,

In others makes the cold too great.
And where these are temperate known,
The soil's all barren sand, or rocky stone.

When once or twice you chanced to view
A rich, well-governed heart,
Like China, it admitted you
But to the frontier-part.
From Paradise shut for evermore,
What good is't that an angel kept the door?

Well fare the pride, and the disdain,
And vanities with beauty joined,
I ne'er had seen this Heart again,
If any fair one had been kind:
My dove, but once let loose, I doubt
Would ne'er return, had not the flood been out.

ABRAHAM COWLEY

The Lost Mistress

All's over, then: does truth sound bitter
As one at first believes?
Hark, 'tis the sparrows' good-night twitter
About your cottage eaves!

And the leaf-buds on the vine are woolly,
I noticed that, today;
One day more bursts them open fully
— You know the red turns grey.

Tomorrow we meet the same then, dearest?
May I take your hand in mine?
Mere friends are we,— well, friends the merest
Keep much that I resign:

For each glance of the eye so bright and black,
Though I keep with heart's endeavour,—
Your voice, when you wish the snowdrops back,
Though it stay in my soul for ever!—

Yet I will but say what mere friends say,
Or only a thought stronger;
I will hold your hand but as long as all may,
Or so very little longer!

ROBERT BROWNING

Surprised by joy—impatient as the wind
I turned to share the transport— O! with whom
But Thee, deep buried in the silent tomb,
That spot which no vicissitude can find?
Love, faithful love, recalled thee to my mind—
But how could I forget thee? Through what power,
Even for the least division of an hour,
Have I been so beguiled as to be blind
To my most grievous loss!—That thought's return
Was the worst pang that sorrow ever bore,
Save one, one only, when I stood forlorn,
Knowing my heart's best treasure was no more;
That neither present time, nor years unborn
Could to my sight that heavenly face restore.

WILLIAM WORDSWORTH

Song

Sweetest love, I do not go
For weariness of thee,
Nor in hope the world can show
A fitter love for me;
But since that I
Must die at last, 'tis best
To use myself in jest
Thus by fained deaths to die.

Yesternight the sun went hence,
And yet is here today,
He hath no desire nor sense,
Nor half so short a way:
Then fear not me,
But believe that I shall make
Speedier journeys, since I take
More wings and spurs than he.

O how feeble is man's power,
That if good fortune fall,
Cannot add another hour,
Nor a lost hour recall!
But come bad chance,

And we join to it our strength,
And we teach it art and length,
Itself o'er us to advance.

When thou sigh'st, thou sigh'st not wind,
  But sigh'st my soul away,
When thou weep'st, unkindly kind,
  My life's blood doth decay.
    It cannot be
That thou lov'st me, as thou say'st,
If in thine my life thou waste,
  Thou art the best of me.

Let not thy divining heart
  Forethink me any ill,
Destiny may take thy part,
  And may thy fears fulfil;
    But think that we
Are but turned aside to sleep;
They who one another keep
Alive, ne'er parted be.

JOHN DONNE

from Modern Love

In our old shipwrecked days there was an hour,
When in the firelight steadily aglow,
Joined slackly, we beheld the red chasm grow
Among the clicking coals. Our library-bower
That eve was left to us: and hushed we sat
As lovers to whom Time is whispering.
From sudden-opened doors we heard them sing:
The nodding elders mixed good wine with chat.
Well knew we that Life's greatest treasure lay
With us, and of it was our talk. 'Ah, yes!
Love dies!' I said: I never thought it less.
She yearned to me that sentence to unsay.
Then when the fire domed blackening, I found
Her cheek was salt against my kiss, and swift
Up the sharp scale of sobs her breast did lift:—
Now am I haunted by that taste! that sound!

At dinner, she is hostess, I am host.
Went the feast ever cheerfuller? She keeps
The Topic over intellectual deeps
In buoyancy afloat. They see no ghost.
With sparkling surface-eyes we ply the ball:
It is in truth a most contagious game:
HIDING THE SKELETON, shall be its name.

Such play as this the devils might appal!
But here's the greater wonder: in that we,
Enamoured of an acting nought can tire,
Each other, like true hypocrites, admire;
Warm-lighted looks, Love's ephemerioe,
Shoot gaily o'er the dishes and the wine.
We waken envy of our happy lot.
Fast, sweet, and golden, shows the marriage-knot.
Dear guests, you now have seen Love's corpse-light
shine.

GEORGE MEREDITH

My life closed twice before its close—
It yet remains to see
If Immortality unveil
A third event to me

So huge, so hopeless to conceive
As these that twice befell.
Parting is all we know of heaven,
And all we need of hell.

EMILY DICKINSON

Song

Ae fond kiss, and then we sever;
Ae fareweel, and then for ever!
Deep in heart-wrung tears I'll pledge thee,
Warring sighs and groans I'll wage thee.—

Who shall say that Fortune grieves him,
While the star of hope she leaves him:
Me, nae chearful twinkle lights me;
Dark despair around benights me.—

I'll ne'er blame my partial fancy,
Naething could resist my Nancy:
But to see her, was to love her;
Love but her, and love for ever.—

Had we never lov'd sae kindly,
Had we never lov'd sae blindly!
Never met— or never parted,
We had ne'er been broken-hearted.—

Fare-thee-weel, thou first and fairest!
Fare-thee-weel, thou best and dearest!
Thine be ilka joy and treasure,
Peace, Enjoyment, Love and Pleasure!—

Ae fond kiss, and then we sever!
Ae fareweel, Alas, for ever!
Deep in heart-wrung tears I'll pledge thee,
Warring sighs and groans I'll wage thee.—

ROBERT BURNS

Down by the Salley Gardens

Down by the salley gardens my love and I did meet;
She passed the salley gardens with little snow-white feet.
She bid me take love easy, as the leaves grow on the tree;
But I, being young and foolish, with her would not agree.

In a field by the river my love and I did stand,
And on my leaning shoulder she laid her snow-white
hand.
She bid me take life easy, as the grass grows on the weirs;
But I was young and foolish, and now am full of tears.

WILLIAM BUTLER YEATS

Cold in the Earth

Cold in the earth—and the deep snow piled above thee,
Far, far removed, cold in the dreary grave!
Have I forgot, my only Love, to love thee,
Severed at last by Time's all-severing wave?

Now, when alone, do my thoughts no longer hover
Over the mountains, on that northern shore,
Resting their wings where heath and fern-leaves cover
Thy noble heart for ever, ever more?

Cold in the earth—and fifteen wild Decembers,
From those brown hills, have melted into spring:
Faithful, indeed, is the spirit that remembers
After such years of change and suffering!

Sweet Love of youth, forgive, if I forget thee,
While the world's tide is bearing me along;
Other desires and other hopes beset me,
Hopes which obscure, but cannot do thee wrong!

No later light has lightened up my heaven,
No second morn has ever shone for me;

All my life's bliss from thy dear life was given,
All my life's bliss is in the grave with thee.

But, when the days of golden dreams had perished,
And even Despair was powerless to destroy;
Then did I learn how existence could be cherished,
Strengthened, and fed without the aid of joy.

Then did I check the tears of useless passion—
Weaned my young soul from yearning after thine;
Sternly denied its burning wish to hasten
Down to that tomb already more than mine.

And, even yet, I dare not let it languish,
Dare not indulge in memory's rapturous pain;
Once drinking deep of that divinest anguish,
How could I seek the empty world again?

EMILY BRONTË

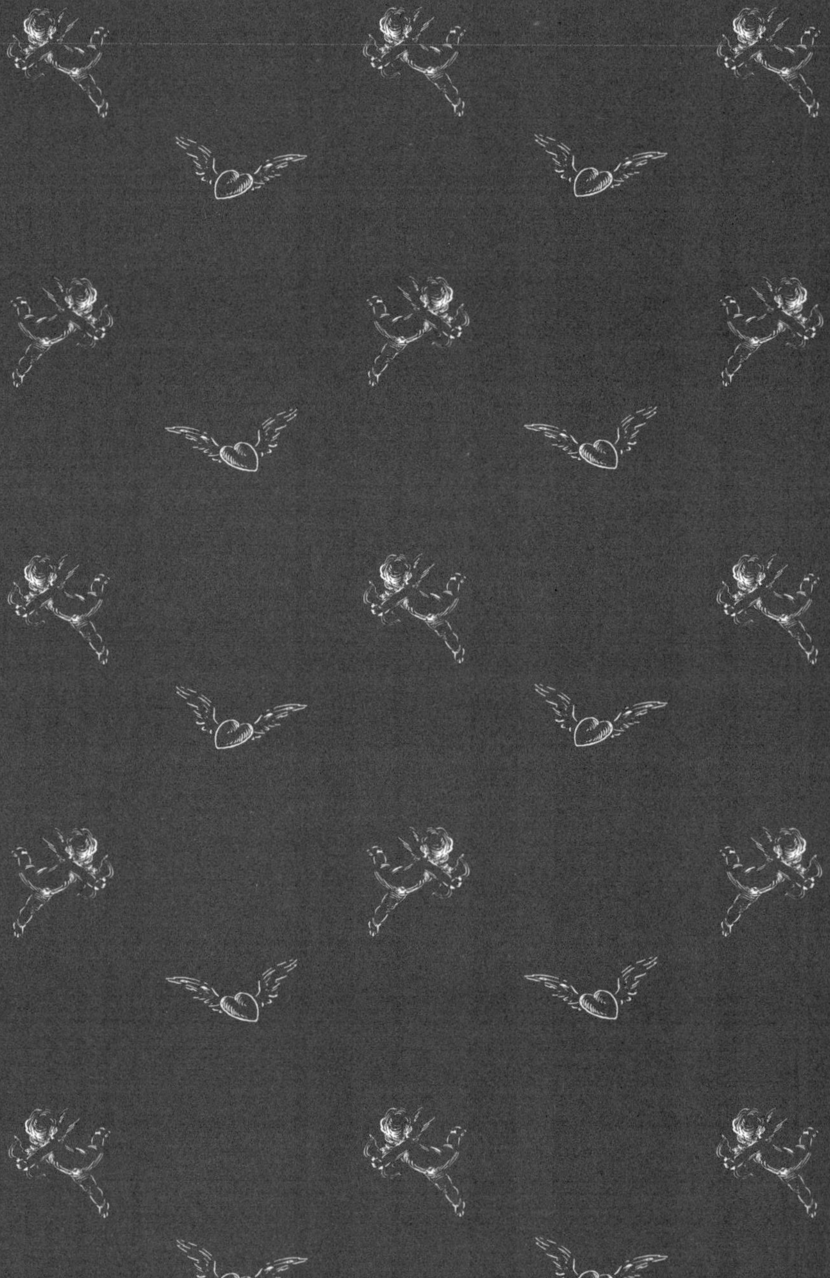